Family
meals

To my children, Nicholas, Lara and Scarlett

ANNABEL KARMEL'S FAVOURITES

Family meals

Quick and easy recipes to keep mealtimes fresh

annabel karmel

1 3 5 7 9 10 8 6 4 2

The Random House Group Limited Reg. No. 954009

A CIP catalogue record for this book is available from the British Library

ISBN: 978-009-195583-0

Printed in Hong Kong

Eddison•Sadd Editions
CREATIVE DIRECTOR Nick Eddison   INDEXER Dorothy Frame
SENIOR EDITOR Katie Golsby   DESIGNER Brazzle Atkins
PROOFREADER Nikky Twyman   ILLUSTRATIONS Nadine Wikenden
PRODUCTION Sarah Rooney

COVER PHOTOGRAPHY Dave King

Notes on the text:
· For fan-assisted ovens, reduce the temperature by 20°C.
· All black pepper is freshly ground.

Contents

Introduction

Ferrying the children to ballet lessons and football practice, keeping up with busy social schedules and a hectic workload – modern lives tend to be extremely busy. Unsurprisingly, for many families, sitting down together to a home-cooked meal can be a rarity.

As a mum of three, I know how hard it can be to juggle work life with keeping a happy family, but rushing around, 'making do' and grabbing food on the go can all lead to unhealthy eating habits, such as snacking, skipping meals, eating fast food and fussy eating.

Even if we do manage to eat meals together at the dinner table, many of us rely on a few fail-safe meals that we cook on rotation. Not only does this reduce the risk of food being left uneaten, but it also takes away the stress of having to think up something new.

Parents often tell me that a lack of inspiration is the reason why they cook the same meals time and time again, but this could mean that your children are missing out on a whole range of nutrients – not to mention an abundance of exciting new tastes and flavours.

Making a success of dinnertime doesn't have to be expensive or time-consuming, and you don't have to be a cordon bleu chef. In this book, you'll find a wonderful selection of recipes to suit the whole family, from comforting classics to exotic ideas from around the world. Created with busy, hungry families in mind, they're fun, easy to prepare and very tasty. Read on for my top tips to help busy mums and dads put the 'mmm' into family mealtimes.

Get organized

This might seem obvious, but organizing the family can be a military operation, so you need to have a finely tuned daily schedule. You'll be surprised by how much this can reduce your stress levels!

When you have time to spare, spend a while planning, cooking and freezing meals for days when you need to produce a meal instantly!

Plan a menu for the week ahead; think about what you can prepare in advance. Get your children involved: if they feel as though they helped with the meal, there's a better chance of them clearing their plates.

Of course, there isn't always time for this, so keep a few quick-fix recipe ideas up your sleeve. Meals that can be rustled up using store-cupboard ingredients are a great back-up.

Savvy shopping

Make a shopping list for the week, and stick to it when you're at the supermarket. This makes it much easier to stick to a budget, and also helps to reduce waste.

Enjoying healthy meals together doesn't need to be expensive: buying seasonal fruit and vegetables can make a big difference to the price, and frozen fruit and vegetables can be cheaper than fresh, but are just as nutritious. Dried and canned lentils and beans are great, too, as they're full of nutrients, ideal for bulking up meals and inexpensive.

Batch cooking

It's a great idea to make more than you need for one mealtime, and freeze the extra portions for a day when you don't have time to cook. It's worth noting that large portions can sometimes overwhelm children, so try freezing small portions in ramekins. Make sure the dishes are thoroughly covered, and label them with their contents and the date the meals were made.

I like to have a list on my freezer that I update whenever I put in or take out a dish, so I know exactly what I have. This way, meals don't get forgotten. There are some guidelines to be aware of when it comes to freezing meals:

- Freeze prepared meals as soon as they are cool.
- Cooked food can be kept in the freezer for up to three months.
- Never refreeze meals that have already been frozen.
- Always reheat food until piping hot.
- Never reheat more than once.

If you have any left-over cooked pasta or potatoes, keep them to supplement another dish later in the week. This will help you to cut down the time you spend in the kitchen, and is another great way to cut down on waste.

Food o'clock

Children like to copy grown-ups, so eating with them is the ideal opportunity to try new foods and practise good table manners. Sitting down together will save time, too.

Sticking to a meal schedule can be tricky, but it's well worth trying to organize at least three or four regular mealtimes during the week, where everyone in the family sits down together. With my children, I found that if they knew when dinner was coming they would be less likely to hunt around for snacks. Whether it's Monday and Friday dinnertime, Saturday breakfast or Sunday lunch, get everyone eating and enjoying 'table time' together. If there *are* occasions when you all have to work to different schedules, this is where your stock of pre-cooked individual portions will come in handy (*see pages 8–9*).

It's good to talk

Family mealtimes offer the perfect opportunity to develop your children's social skills. Interacting and discussing the day's events will develop their listening and conversational skills and give you a chance to reconnect as a family. This is especially important if you're very busy. Try to keep the TV switched off during meals. If it's on, you can guarantee children will watch it rather than engage in conversation.

The benefits of family meals

From a very early age, children need a routine. Being involved in family mealtimes from the start will help your child to understand and appreciate the importance of eating together as a family unit.

Eating healthily is also crucial, setting a dietary pattern for life and reducing the risk of diet-related diseases. A varied, well-balanced diet will provide your child with all the essential nutrients, minerals and vitamins she needs to grow and develop. What's more, eating well from a young age will discourage fussy eating.

Variety and inspiration

Many of the recipes in this book have been inspired by flavours from around the world. Most of the ingredients I've used for these recipes are widely available, so it's easy to find your adventurous side.

You'll be surprised by the flavours your child enjoys. My noodle recipes went down a treat with my children when they were young, especially when I supplied them with child-friendly chopsticks (*see page 41*). It's important that children have fun with food. Another trick is to turn your meal into a talking point by finding the origin of a dish on a map.

Recipe information

The recipes in this book are accompanied by helpful information on preparation and cooking times, how many portions the recipe makes and whether it's suitable for freezing. Preparation times and portion quantities should be used as a guide only, as these will vary.

I hope my handy book of family meals brings you and your children to the dinner table for some well-deserved family time. Enjoy it.

Vegetables

Tomato and cheese quesadilla

Heat the oil in a small frying pan and add the onion and tomato. Sauté for 3–4 minutes, until the tomatoes are soft. Remove from the heat, stir in the Tabasco sauce and season to taste.

Heat a large griddle or non-stick frying pan. Spread the tomato mixture over one tortilla and scatter over the cheese. Sandwich with the second tortilla and heat in the hot pan for 2–3 minutes on each side, until the cheese has melted. Transfer to a chopping board and cut into 12 wedges.

🍴 10 MINUTES

🔲 10 MINUTES

🍴 2 PORTIONS

❄ NOT SUITABLE FOR FREEZING

1 teaspoon sunflower oil
2 spring onions, thinly sliced
6 large, or 10 small, cherry tomatoes, roughly chopped
3–4 drops of Tabasco sauce
salt and pepper
2 flour tortillas
55 g (2 oz) Cheddar cheese, grated

Tomatoes contain lycopene, a powerful pigment that's important in the prevention of cancer. Men who have a high level of lycopene in their fat stores reduce the risk of having a heart attack by half.

Caramelized red onion and mozzarella wraps

🔪 10 MINUTES

▦ 25 MINUTES

🍳 2 PORTIONS

❄ NOT SUITABLE FOR FREEZING

1 tablespoon olive oil, plus
    ½ teaspoon for dressing
2 medium red onions,
    peeled and thinly sliced
1½ teaspoons chopped
    thyme
2 teaspoons brown sugar
2 teaspoons balsamic
    vinegar, plus a few drops
    for dressing
salt and pepper
2 flour tortillas
125 g (4½ oz) mozzarella
    cheese, sliced
a handful of rocket leaves
    (about 20 g/¾ oz)

Heat 1 tablespoon of oil in a non-stick frying pan, add the onion and thyme and fry over a low heat for 15 minutes, stirring regularly. Mix in the sugar, balsamic vinegar and seasoning and continue to cook for 5 minutes. Turn up the heat and cook for 1 minute, until all the liquid has evaporated. Remove from the heat and leave to cool.

Heat the tortillas according to the packet instructions, either in a microwave or dry frying pan. Divide the onion mixture between them, then lay the slices of mozzarella on top, and season.

Toss the rocket leaves with the remaining oil and balsamic vinegar, and place on top of the mozzarella. Roll up the tortillas, then cut in half diagonally and serve.

Wraps are fun to make and children love helping to arrange the fillings and roll up the tortillas. I find that when children are involved in making their food they tend to enjoy eating it more.

Tomato and vegetable soup

Heat the oil in a saucepan and add the onion, celery, pepper and carrot. Sauté for 5 minutes, then add the garlic and thyme and cook for another 2 minutes. Add the tinned tomatoes, stock, tomato purée and sugar. Season to taste and bring to the boil, then cover and simmer for 10–15 minutes, until all the vegetables are tender.

Leave the soup to cool for about 5 minutes, then blend until smooth using an electric hand blender or food processor. Finally, swirl in the cream and serve.

🖊 15 MINUTES

▭ 30–35 MINUTES

🕐 4 PORTIONS

❄ SUITABLE FOR FREEZING

1 tablespoon olive oil
1 large onion, peeled and chopped
2 sticks celery, chopped
1 red pepper, deseeded and chopped
1 carrot, peeled and grated
1 garlic clove, crushed
1 teaspoon chopped thyme
400 g (14 oz) tinned chopped tomatoes
450 ml (¾ pint) chicken or vegetable stock
1½ tablespoons tomato purée
a pinch of sugar
salt and pepper
2 tablespoons double cream

Spiced lentil soup

🔪 5 MINUTES

🍳 30 MINUTES

🕐 4 PORTIONS

❄ SUITABLE FOR FREEZING

1 tablespoon olive oil
1 red onion, peeled and
    chopped
2 small carrots, peeled and
    chopped
1 garlic clove, crushed
½ red chilli, deseeded and
    chopped
40 g (1½ oz) red lentils
½ teaspoon ground cumin
½ teaspoon ground
    coriander
400 g (14 oz) tinned
    chopped tomatoes
600 ml (1 pint) vegetable
    stock
1 tablespoon tomato purée
1 teaspoon mango chutney

Heat the oil in a saucepan and add the onion, carrot, garlic and chilli. Fry for 5 minutes, then add the lentils, spices, tomatoes, stock, tomato purée and mango chutney. Bring to the boil, then cover and simmer for 20 minutes, until the lentils and vegetables are tender.

Lentils are a good non-meat source of iron.

Butternut squash and pea risotto

Preheat the oven to 220°C/430°F/Gas 7.

Put the butternut squash onto a baking sheet, toss in 1 tablespoon of the oil and season. Roast in the oven for 25 minutes, until golden brown.

Meanwhile, pour the chicken stock into a saucepan, bring to the boil, then reduce the heat to low.

Heat the remaining oil in a saucepan, add the onion and garlic and stir over the heat for 2-3 minutes. Add the rice and coat in the mixture. Add a ladleful of stock to the rice, along with the white wine. Stir until the liquid is absorbed, then continue to add ladles of stock until the rice is cooked, adding the peas about 5 minutes before the end of the cooking time.

Add the butternut squash, Parmesan, lemon juice and parsley, and season well. Serve immediately.

🖊 10 MINUTES

🗔 25–30 MINUTES

🍳 4 PORTIONS

❄ NOT SUITABLE FOR FREEZING

250 g (9 oz) butternut squash, peeled, deseeded and cubed
3 tablespoons olive oil
salt and pepper
750 ml (1¼ pints) chicken stock
1 large onion, peeled and roughly chopped
2 garlic cloves, crushed
175 g (6 oz) risotto rice
75 ml (2½ fl oz) white wine
100 g (3½ oz) frozen peas
25 g (1 oz) Parmesan cheese, grated
1 teaspoon lemon juice
1 tablespoon chopped parsley

My favourite pizza

First, make the dough. Put all the dough ingredients in a large bowl and mix together until they form a ball. Transfer to a floured work surface and knead for 5 minutes. Place the dough in an oiled bowl, cover with clingfilm and leave to prove for 1 hour.

Meanwhile, make the sauce. Heat the oil in a saucepan and add the onion, garlic, pepper and courgette. Fry for 5 minutes, then add the tinned tomatoes, tomato purée and sugar. Bring to the boil, then simmer for 15 minutes, until the vegetables are soft and the sauce is thick. Whiz until smooth using an electric hand blender.

Preheat the oven to 220°C/430°F/Gas 7. Roll out the dough to form a large circle (about 28 cm/ 11 in in diameter), then transfer to a baking sheet. Spread over the tomato sauce and top with the sliced tomato and cheeses. Sprinkle over the basil. Bake for 15–18 minutes, until the base has risen and the topping is golden brown.

✎ 30 MINUTES, PLUS 1 HOUR FOR PROVING

▦ 20 MINUTES

🍰 8 SLICES

❄ SUITABLE FOR FREEZING

1 tablespoon olive oil
1 onion, peeled and finely chopped
2 garlic cloves, crushed
½ red pepper, deseeded and diced
½ courgette, diced
400 g (14 oz) tinned chopped tomatoes
3 tablespoons tomato purée
a pinch of sugar
4 plum tomatoes, sliced
100 g (3½ oz) Cheddar cheese, grated
425 g (15 oz) mozzarella cheese, sliced
a few basil leaves, chopped

Dough
250 g (9 oz) strong white flour
1½ teaspoons dried yeast
½ teaspoon salt
200 ml (7 fl oz) water
1 tablespoon olive oil

Yummy vegetable cashew burgers

🔪 25 MINUTES, PLUS 1 HOUR
FOR CHILLING

🍳 12 MINUTES

🍔 8 SMALL BURGERS

❄️ SUITABLE FOR FREEZING
(BEFORE FINAL FRYING STAGE)

100 g (3½ oz) unsalted
cashew nuts
1 tablespoon olive oil
1 red onion, peeled and
chopped
1 carrot, peeled and grated
½ small leek, chopped
100 g (3½ oz) mushrooms,
sliced
1 garlic clove, crushed
¼ teaspoon thyme leaves
50 g/2 oz brown rice, cooked
1 tablespoon dark soy sauce
40 g (1½ oz) Gruyère cheese,
grated
50 g (2 oz) fresh breadcrumbs
1 tablespoon clear honey
1 egg yolk
salt and pepper
plain flour, for dusting
2 tablespoons sunflower oil,
for frying

Preheat the oven to 180°C/350°F/Gas 4. Spread the cashew nuts on a baking sheet and roast for 8–10 minutes. Watch them carefully, as after about 5 minutes they will brown quickly. Alternatively, you can buy unsalted, roasted cashew nuts.

Heat the oil in a large frying pan with the onion, carrot, leek, mushrooms, garlic and thyme. Sauté for 10 minutes, until the vegetables are soft and the liquid has evaporated. Add the cooked rice and cook for 1 minute. Allow to cool slightly.

Put the cashew nuts in a food processor and pulse 6 or 7 times, until coarsely chopped. Add the rice mixture, along with the soy sauce, Gruyère, breadcrumbs, honey, egg yolk and seasoning, and pulse 5 or 6 times until just combined.

With floured hands, form the mixture into 8 patties (it will be a bit wet). Refrigerate for at least an hour, or overnight.

Dust the burgers with flour, heat the sunflower oil in a non-stick frying pan and fry over a low heat for about 3 minutes on each side.

Fish

Lemon sole with vegetables in a Chinese sauce

⌁ 15 MINUTES

▦ 20–25 MINUTES

◉ 4 PORTIONS

❋ NOT SUITABLE FOR FREEZING

First, season the lemon sole with salt and pepper. Toss the fish in the flour, then dip it in the egg and coat in the breadcrumbs.

Next, make the sauce. In a saucepan, mix the cornflour with the water. Add the remaining ingredients, bring to the boil and stir until thickened.

Heat a little oil in a frying pan, and fry the lemon sole for 3–4 minutes on each side, until lightly golden and cooked through. Transfer to a plate and keep warm.

Heat 1 tablespoon of oil in the frying pan. Add the onion and fry for 3 minutes. Add the pepper and courgette to the pan and fry until just softened. Season to taste.

Arrange the vegetables in a dish, place the fish on top and pour over the hot sauce.

3 large lemon sole fillets, skinned and cut into 8 strips per fillet
salt and pepper
50 g (2 oz) plain flour
1 egg, beaten
50 g (2 oz) Panko breadcrumbs
sunflower oil, for frying
1 onion, peeled and thinly sliced
½ red pepper, deseeded and sliced
1 courgette, topped and tailed, and sliced into strips

Chinese sauce
1 tablespoon cornflour
2 tablespoons water
300 ml (½ pint) chicken stock
1 tablespoon caster sugar
2 teaspoons soy sauce
1 tablespoon sweet chilli sauce
1 teaspoon rice wine vinegar
½ teaspoon sesame oil

Simply super salmon teriyaki

🔪 5 MINUTES
🍳 20 MINUTES
🍽 4 PORTIONS
❄ NOT SUITABLE FOR FREEZING

4 x 150 g (5 oz) thick salmon
    fillets, skinned
1–2 tablespoons vegetable
    oil
150 g (5 oz) button
    mushrooms, sliced
150 g (5 oz) beansprouts

Teriyaki marinade
80 ml (3 fl oz) soy sauce
100 ml (3½ fl oz) sake
50 ml (2 fl oz) mirin (sweet
    sake for cooking)
2 tablespoons sugar

Combine the marinade ingredients in a saucepan and stir over a medium heat until the sugar has dissolved. Add the salmon and marinate for 10 minutes.

Heat 1 tablespoon of oil in a saucepan and sauté the mushrooms for 2 minutes, then add the beansprouts and cook for another 2 minutes.

Meanwhile, drain the salmon, reserving the marinade. Brush a very hot griddle pan with a little oil and cook the salmon for 1–2 minutes on each side, or until beginning to brown. Alternatively, heat in a frying pan with 1 tablespoon of oil. When the salmon is cooked, pour away the excess oil from the pan.

Pour a little of the teriyaki marinade over the salmon and continue to cook for a few minutes, basting occasionally. Put the remaining marinade in a small saucepan and simmer until thickened.

Divide the mushrooms and beansprouts between four plates, place the salmon on top and pour over the teriyaki sauce. Serve with basmati rice.

Fish pie with rösti topping

Preheat the oven to 200°C/400°F/Gas 6. Cook the potatoes in boiling salted water until just tender. Drain and leave to cool a little.

Melt the butter in a saucepan, add the leeks and sauté until softened. Add the rice wine vinegar and flour, then blend in the milk, stirring until thickened. Add the Dijon mustard and Parmesan, followed by the cod, salmon and chives. Spoon into an ovenproof dish.

Grate the potatoes over the top of the fish and drizzle over the melted butter. Bake for 30–35 minutes, until bubbling and lightly golden.

⏲ 15 MINUTES
🗔 55–60 MINUTES
🕐 4–6 PORTIONS
❄ SUITABLE FOR FREEZING

1 kg (2 lb 3 oz) potatoes, peeled and cut into chunks
50 g (2 oz) butter
2 leeks, sliced
1 tablespoon rice wine vinegar
50 g (2 oz) plain flour
550 ml (19 fl oz) milk
1 teaspoon Dijon mustard
50 g (2 oz) Parmesan cheese, grated
250 g (9 oz) cod fillet, skinned and cut into chunks
250 g (9 oz) salmon fillet, skinned and cut into chunks
2 tablespoons chopped chives
a little butter, melted

Cod fillets with tomato salsa

✎ 5 MINUTES

▦ 20 MINUTES

⏲ 4 PORTIONS

❄ SUITABLE FOR FREEZING

4 x 125 g (4½ oz) cod fillets, skinned
olive oil, for brushing
salt and pepper
50 g (2 oz) white breadcrumbs
1 tablespoon snipped chives
¼ teaspoon lemon zest
25 g (1 oz) Parmesan cheese, grated
paprika, for topping

Salsa
2 tomatoes, deseeded and diced
2 spring onions, sliced
1 tablespoon chopped chives
1 tablespoon chopped basil
1 tablespoon rice wine vinegar
2 tablespoons olive oil
a pinch of sugar

Preheat the oven to 200°C/400°F/Gas 6.

Put the cod fillets on a greased baking sheet, brush with the oil and season. Combine the breadcrumbs, chives, lemon zest and Parmesan and sprinkle over the cod. Top with paprika.

Bake for 10 minutes, until just cooked, lightly golden and crisp.

Mix together all the salsa ingredients and serve with the fish.

Mild king prawn curry

🔪 5 MINUTES

📟 35 MINUTES

🍳 4 PORTIONS

❄️ SUITABLE FOR FREEZING

1 tablespoon sunflower oil
1 large onion, peeled and
  finely chopped
1 large garlic clove, crushed
½ green chilli, deseeded and
  finely chopped
1 red pepper, deseeded and
  finely chopped
1 tablespoon garam masala
  powder
400 g (14 oz) tinned
  chopped tomatoes
260 ml (9 fl oz) water
50 g (2 oz) creamed coconut
1 tablespoon tomato purée
1 tablespoon mango
  chutney
450 g (1 lb) raw king prawns
salt and pepper

Heat the oil in a large saucepan. Fry the onion, garlic, chilli and red pepper for 5 minutes, until almost soft. Add the garam masala and stir until the onion mixture is coated. Add the tinned tomatoes, water, creamed coconut, tomato purée and mango chutney. Bring to the boil, cover and simmer for 20 minutes.

Add the prawns to the pan and stir until the prawns turn pink and are cooked through. Season with salt and pepper and serve with rice.

Prawns are rich in selenium and zinc, which we need in order to maintain a strong immune system. Zinc is also important for repair and healing.

Tuna tagliatelle

/ 15 MINUTES

▭ 40 MINUTES

◉ 6 PORTIONS

✳ SUITABLE FOR FREEZING

Preheat the oven to 180°C/350°F/Gas 4. Cook the tagliatelle according to the packet instructions, until just tender.

Melt 25 g (1 oz) of butter in a saucepan and sauté the onion until soft. Mix the cornflour and water to form a smooth paste. Add to the pan with the soup and herbs, and cook over a medium heat for about 5 minutes, or until the sauce has thickened. Stir in the tuna and mix with the tagliatelle.

Next, make a cheese sauce. Put the remaining 25 g (1 oz) butter into a saucepan with the flour and milk, and whisk over a medium heat until it boils and becomes thick and smooth. Stir in the mustard powder and simmer for 2–3 minutes. Remove from the heat and stir in 75 g (3 oz) of the Cheddar, until melted. Stir in the chives and sweetcorn and season to taste.

Tip the tuna mixture into an ovenproof dish measuring 25 x 20 cm (10 x 8 in) and pour over the cheese sauce. Mix together the breadcrumbs, remaining Cheddar and the Parmesan and scatter over the top. Cook in the oven for 20 minutes, then brown under a hot grill for a few minutes before serving.

225 g (8 oz) green and white tagliatelle
50 g (2 oz) butter
1 small onion, peeled and finely chopped
1 heaped tablespoon cornflour
2 tablespoons cold water
400 g (14 oz) cream of tomato soup
2 tablespoons chopped parsley
1 teaspoon dried mixed herbs
400 g (14 oz) tinned tuna, drained
20 g (3/4 oz) flour
375 ml (13 fl oz) milk
a pinch of mustard powder
100 g (3 1/2 oz) Cheddar cheese, grated
1 tablespoon snipped chives
50 g (2 oz) sweetcorn, cooked
salt and pepper
25 g (1 oz) brown breadcrumbs
1 tablespoon grated Parmesan cheese

Prawn and tomato spaghetti

Cook the spaghetti according to the packet instructions, then drain.

Meanwhile, heat the oil in a saucepan. Add the onion and garlic and fry for 3 minutes, then add the sugar, tomato purée and tomatoes. Bring to the boil, then simmer for 10 minutes until the tomatoes are soft. Add the basil and parsley.

Melt the butter in a frying pan. Add the prawns and fry until pink. Add the tomato sauce and spaghetti, then add the lemon juice and season well.

To remove the skin from a tomato, cut a cross in the base using a sharp knife. Put in a bowl and cover with boiling water. Leave for 1 minute. Drain and rinse in cold water. The skin should peel off easily.

🖊 10 MINUTES

🍳 20 MINUTES

🥘 4 PORTIONS

❄ NOT SUITABLE FOR FREEZING

225 g (8 oz) spaghetti
1 tablespoon olive oil
1 onion, peeled and chopped
2 garlic cloves, crushed
2 teaspoons caster sugar
1 tablespoon tomato purée
8 plum tomatoes, skinned (*see box, left*) and quartered
2 tablespoons chopped basil
1 tablespoon chopped parsley
a knob of butter
250 g (9 oz) raw prawns, peeled
juice of ½ a small lemon
salt and pepper

Chicken

Tasty chicken and potato pie

🖉 20 MINUTES

⬛ 50 MINUTES

🍽 4 PORTIONS

❄ SUITABLE FOR FREEZING

Preheat the oven to 200°C/400°F/Gas 6. Put the potatoes in cold, salted water, bring to the boil, then reduce the heat and simmer for 10–15 minutes, until tender.

Meanwhile, melt 25 g (1 oz) of the butter in a saucepan and cook the leek and shallot over a low heat for 8–10 minutes, until soft but not coloured. Stir in the flour and cook for 1 minute, then stir in the stock, a little at a time, to make a smooth sauce (you may find it easier to do this off the heat). Stir in the cream, then cook, stirring, until the sauce just comes to the boil. Stir in the chicken, peas and parsley, then remove from the heat and stir in the lemon juice. Season to taste.

Drain the potatoes, and mash with the remaining butter, plus the milk and cheeses. Spoon the chicken into a 1.5 litre (2½ pint) dish and top with the mash.

Bake for about 30 minutes until golden brown (it will need longer if cooking from chilled). It's a good idea to place the dish on a baking sheet, to catch any drips.

500 g (1 lb 2 oz) potatoes, peeled and cut into chunks
50 g (2 oz) butter
1 leek, thinly sliced
1 large, or 2 small, shallots, peeled and finely chopped
25 g (1 oz) plain flour
300 ml (½ pint) chicken stock
100 ml (3½ fl oz) double cream
300 g (11 oz) shredded cooked chicken
75 g (3 oz) frozen peas
1 tablespoon chopped parsley
1 tablespoon lemon juice
salt and pepper
100 ml (3½ fl oz) milk
50 g (2 oz) Cheddar cheese, grated
15 g (½ oz) Parmesan cheese, grated

Marinated griddled chicken with stir-fried vegetables

⟋ 20 MINUTES, PLUS 1 HOUR
FOR MARINATING

▦ 20 MINUTES

⊛ 6 PORTIONS

✳ SUITABLE FOR FREEZING

4 small chicken breast fillets
salt and pepper
1 tablespoon cornflour
150 ml (¼ pint) chicken stock
1–2 tablespoons olive oil
1 carrot, peeled and cut into
    thin strips
1 onion, peeled and chopped
1 courgette, cut into strips
½ red pepper, deseeded and
    sliced
1 garlic clove, crushed

Marinade
1 garlic clove, crushed
1 teaspoon fresh root ginger,
    grated
juice of 1 large orange
1 tablespoon olive oil
1 tablespoon soy sauce
1 tablespoon honey

First, make the marinade. Put all the marinade ingredients into a bowl and combine.

Cover the chicken breasts with clingfilm and bash with a mallet, so that they're all the same thickness. Mix into the marinade and leave for at least 1 hour, or overnight if possible.

Remove the chicken (reserving the marinade), then season. Brush a hot griddle pan with a little oil, and fry the chicken for 3–4 minutes on each side, until golden and cooked through. Cut the chicken into pieces.

Mix the cornflour with the marinade, pour into a saucepan and add the stock. Bring to the boil, stirring until thickened and bubbling.

Heat 1 tablespoon of oil in a frying pan, add the carrot and onion, and fry for 3 minutes. Add the courgette, pepper and garlic, and fry for another 3 minutes. Season well and arrange in a dish. Place the chicken on top and pour over the sauce.

Roast chicken and herb stuffing

✐ 15 MINUTES

⊞ 2–2½ HOURS

◷ 4–6 PORTIONS

✳ NOT SUITABLE FOR FREEZING

Preheat the oven to 220°C/430°F/Gas 7. Rub olive oil over the chicken, then squeeze over some lemon juice and put the remaining lemon inside the cavity with the onion and herbs. Season to taste. Put the chicken in a roasting tin and roast for 20 minutes per 500 g (1 lb), plus 20 minutes extra.

To make the stuffing, heat the sunflower oil and sauté the onions for 5–6 minutes. Add the remaining ingredients and season. Spoon into a greased dish and bake for 25–30 minutes, until golden and crisp.

Put the cooked chicken on a plate and keep warm. Add flour to the juices in the tin, heat on the hob and stir, then blend in the stock, Worcestershire sauce and sugar. Heat through and sieve into a jug.

olive oil
1 medium chicken
1 lemon
½ onion
a few sprigs of thyme
a few sprigs of sage
salt and pepper

Stuffing
2 tablespoons sunflower oil
3 medium onions, peeled and chopped
200 g (7 oz) coarse fresh breadcrumbs
1 tablespoon chopped sage
1 tablespoon chopped thyme
1 tablespoon chopped chives
100 ml (3½ fl oz) olive oil

Gravy
2 tablespoons plain flour
600 ml (1 pint) chicken stock
1 teaspoon Worcestershire sauce
a pinch of sugar

Chicken casserole

🔪 10 MINUTES

📅 20 MINUTES

🍽 4–6 PORTIONS

❄ SUITABLE FOR FREEZING

2 tablespoons olive oil
4 chicken breast fillets,
   thickly sliced
1 tablespoon runny honey
salt and pepper
25 g (1 oz) butter
1 large onion, peeled and
   chopped
1 medium carrot, peeled,
   halved lengthways and
   sliced
1 garlic clove, crushed
2 tablespoons flour
150 ml (¼ pint) white wine
200 ml (7 fl oz) chicken stock
75 g (3 oz) frozen peas
75 g (3 oz) broccoli florets
4 tablespoons crème fraîche
1 tablespoon tarragon
a pinch of sugar

First, toss the oil with the chicken, then add the honey and seasoning. Fry the chicken for a few minutes, until golden, then set aside.

Heat the butter in a saucepan, then add the onion and carrot. Cover and allow to cook gently for 5 minutes, until softened. Add the garlic, then stir in the flour. Blend in the wine and stock, then bring to the boil. Add the chicken, cover and simmer for 5 minutes.

Cook the peas and broccoli in boiling water for 3–4 minutes, then drain.

Add the crème fraîche, tarragon and sugar to the chicken casserole, then stir in the peas and broccoli. Season to taste, and serve.

Monounsaturated oils such as olive oil can help to lower blood cholesterol levels. Olive oil is also a good source of vitamin E.

Sweet and sour chicken

🔪 15 MINUTES

▦ 15 MINUTES

🕚 4 PORTIONS

❄ NOT SUITABLE FOR FREEZING

In a small bowl, beat together the egg yolk, cornflour and milk to make a thin batter. Heat 2 tablespoons of vegetable oil in a wok, then dip the chicken into the batter and fry for 3–4 minutes, until golden. Remove from the wok and set aside.

Mix together all the ingredients for the sweet and sour sauce. Heat the remaining vegetable oil in a wok and stir-fry the carrot, baby corn and green beans for 2 minutes. Add the sauce, bring to the boil and cook for 2 minutes. Remove from the heat and stir in the spring onions. Add the chicken to the vegetables and heat through. Season to taste and serve with fluffy white rice.

1 egg yolk
1½ tablespoons cornflour
1 tablespoon milk
4 tablespoons vegetable oil
250 g (9 oz) chicken breasts, cut into bite-size chunks
75 g (3 oz) carrot, peeled and cut into matchsticks
50 g (2 oz) baby corn, sliced in half lengthways, then across
50 g (2 oz) fine green beans, topped and tailed, and cut in half
2 spring onions, finely sliced
salt and pepper

Sweet and sour sauce

1 tablespoon soy sauce
2 tablespoons tomato ketchup
2 tablespoons rice wine vinegar
2 tablespoons caster sugar
½ teaspoon sesame oil

You can buy child-friendly plastic chopsticks, which are joined at the top so that they only need to be squeezed together to pick up food. These can make mealtimes great fun, and this recipe would be perfect for trying them out, as everything is cut into bite-size pieces.

Chicken satay

10 MINUTES, PLUS 30 MINUTES FOR MARINATING

10 MINUTES

2 PORTIONS

NOT SUITABLE FOR FREEZING

2 garlic cloves, peeled
1 tablespoon chopped fresh root ginger
3 tablespoons smooth peanut butter
2 tablespoons rice wine vinegar
3 tablespoons light soy sauce
3 tablespoons dark brown sugar
1 small chilli, deseeded
3 tablespoons lime juice
1 small shallot
salt and pepper
1 tablespoon groundnut oil
2 chicken breasts, cut into strips
sweet chilli sauce, to serve (optional)

Put all the ingredients except the groundnut oil, chicken and sweet chilli sauce into a mini food processor, and blend until smooth. Transfer to a bowl, add the chicken and marinate for a minimum of 30 minutes, or up to 4 hours – the longer, the better.

Heat the groundnut oil in a frying pan. Remove the chicken from the marinade and fry until it's cooked through and the surface has caramelized. Alternatively, the chicken can be put on to skewers and barbecued.

Serve with a dipping sauce, such as sweet chilli sauce.

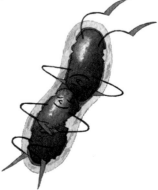

Fruity chicken curry

🔪 10 MINUTES

📅 25 MINUTES

🍳 2 PORTIONS

❄ SUITABLE FOR FREEZING

2 tablespoons vegetable oil
1 onion, peeled and chopped
1 medium carrot, peeled and
   cut into matchsticks
1 garlic clove, crushed
1 medium apple, peeled,
   cored and thinly sliced
350 g (12 oz) chicken breast
   fillets, cut into bite-size
   chunks
1 tablespoon Korma curry
   paste
½ tablespoon mango
   chutney
1 tablespoon tomato purée
150 ml (¼ pint) coconut milk
150 ml (¼ pint) chicken stock
100 g (3½ oz) frozen peas
salt and pepper

Heat the oil in a wok or frying pan and sauté the onion and carrot for 3 minutes. Add the garlic and sauté for 30 seconds, then add the apple and stir-fry for 3 minutes. Add the chicken and stir-fry for another 4 minutes.

Add the curry paste, mango chutney, tomato purée, coconut milk and chicken stock, and simmer for about 7 minutes. Add the peas and cook for another 3 minutes.

Season to taste, and serve with fluffy white rice and poppadums.

If you wish, you could add some baby corn to this delicious mild curry recipe.

Thai chicken soup

Heat the oil in a saucepan, then add the onion, chilli and ginger. Fry until softened, then add the curry paste and flour, and blend in the coconut milk and stock. Add the fish sauce and sugar, then bring to the boil and simmer for 5 minutes. Stir in the chicken.

Cook the noodles and broccoli in boiling water for 4 minutes. Drain, then add to the soup.

🖊 5 MINUTES

🍳 20 MINUTES

🥧 3 PORTIONS

❄ SUITABLE FOR FREEZING

1 tablespoon sunflower oil
1 onion, peeled and finely chopped
½ red chilli, deseeded and chopped
½ teaspoon grated fresh root ginger
1 tablespoon Thai red curry paste
1 tablespoon plain flour
400 ml (14 fl oz) coconut milk
300 ml (½ pint) chicken stock
1 teaspoon fish sauce
2 teaspoons brown sugar
30 g (1 oz) chicken breast, cooked and sliced
20 g (¾ oz) fine egg noodles
30 g (1 oz) broccoli florets

Ginger aids digestion and is a good remedy for nausea, particularly travel sickness.

Thai chicken with butternut squash

Heat 1 tablespoon of the oil in a saucepan. Add the onion, ginger and garlic and sauté over a low heat for 8–10 minutes, until softened. Add the curry paste and flour and fry for 1 minute. Blend in the coconut milk, stock or water, fish sauce, sugar and lime zest and juice. Bring to the boil and simmer for 5 minutes. Add the lemongrass and butternut squash, then cover and simmer for another 5 minutes.

Heat the remaining oil in a frying pan and brown the chicken, then add to the sauce and simmer for 5–6 minutes, until cooked through. Remove the lemongrass.

Add the spring onions and garnish with coriander leaves. Serve with jasmine rice and mini poppadums.

15 MINUTES

35–40 MINUTES

2 PORTIONS

SUITABLE FOR FREEZING

2 tablespoons sunflower oil
2 onions, peeled and sliced
15 g (½ oz) fresh root ginger, peeled and crushed
1 garlic clove, crushed
2 tablespoons Thai red curry paste
1½ tablespoons plain flour
400 ml (14 fl oz) coconut milk
300 ml (½ pint) chicken stock or water
2–3 teaspoons fish sauce
2 teaspoons brown sugar
zest and juice of ½ a lime
½ lemongrass stalk, bashed
110 g (4 oz) butternut squash, peeled, deseeded and diced
2 chicken breasts, cut into chunks
2 spring onions, sliced
coriander leaves, to garnish

Delicious chicken fajitas

✏️ 5 MINUTES

🍳 30–35 MINUTES

🍽️ 8 FAJITAS

❄️ SUITABLE FOR FREEZING

2 small chicken breast
   fillets, cut into strips
a pinch of paprika
a pinch of mild chilli
   powder
a pinch of cumin (optional)
a pinch of oregano
1 tablespoon olive oil, plus 1
   teaspoon
1 garlic clove, crushed
1 onion, peeled and thinly
   sliced
½ small red pepper,
   deseeded and thinly sliced
salt and pepper
8 small flour tortillas
75 g (3 oz) iceberg lettuce,
   shredded
75 g (3 oz) Cheddar cheese,
   grated
3 tablespoons sour cream

Toss the chicken in the paprika, chilli powder, cumin (if using) and oregano. Heat 1 teaspoon of the oil in a frying pan and sauté the chicken, stirring occasionally, for 3–4 minutes. Remove the chicken with a slotted spoon and set aside.

Add the remaining tablespoon of oil to the pan and sauté the garlic, onion and red pepper for 5 minutes. Return the chicken to the pan, season to taste and heat through.

To make the tomato salsa (*for ingredients, see right*), heat the oil and fry the chilli, onion, green pepper and garlic for about 5 minutes. Add the vinegar and cook for about 20 seconds, then add the tinned tomatoes, seasoning and parsley. Simmer, uncovered, for about 15 minutes.

Heat the tortillas in the microwave according to the packet instructions. Then, to assemble the fajitas, place some of the chicken mixture along the centre of each tortilla, top with some tomato salsa, lettuce, Cheddar and a little sour cream, and roll up.

Tomato salsa

½ tablespoon olive oil
¼ green chilli, deseeded and finely sliced
½ onion, peeled and chopped
¼ small green pepper, deseeded and chopped
1 small garlic clove, crushed
½ teaspoon red wine vinegar
200 g (7 oz) tinned chopped tomatoes
salt and pepper
½ tablespoon parsley

Chicken yakitori with noodles

🖋 15 MINUTES, PLUS 30 MINUTES
FOR MARINATING

🍳 20 MINUTES

🍽 3 PORTIONS

❄ NOT SUITABLE FOR FREEZING

Preheat the oven to 220°C/430°F/Gas 7. Put the mirin, honey, soy sauce, vinegar, ginger and garlic into a small pan. Bring to the boil and stir until reduced by a third. Leave to cool.

When cold, mix the marinade with the chicken and marinate for 30 minutes. Season and thread onto the skewers.

Heat 2 tablespoons of the oil in a frying pan, and cook the chicken for 2–3 minutes on each side, until golden. Place the chicken skewers on a baking sheet, then cook in the oven for 12–15 minutes, until cooked through.

Meanwhile, cook the noodles according to the packet instructions, and drain.

Heat the remaining oil in a frying pan or wok. Fry all the vegetables for 3–4 minutes, then add the noodles, along with the stock, soy sauce and sweet chilli sauce. Season to taste, and heat through. Serve with the kebabs.

3 tablespoons mirin
3 tablespoons honey
3 tablespoons soy sauce
2 teaspoons rice wine vinegar
1 teaspoon grated fresh root
  ginger
1 garlic clove, crushed
4 chicken thighs, filleted
  and cut into large chunks
salt and pepper
3 tablespoons sunflower oil
125 g (4½ oz) medium noodles
1 large courgette, cut into
  sticks
1 large carrot, peeled and
  cut into sticks
2 spring onions, thinly sliced
1 red onion, peeled and sliced
75 g (3 oz) chestnut
  mushrooms, sliced
75 ml (2½ fl oz) chicken stock
4 teaspoons soy sauce
4 teaspoons sweet chilli sauce
6 bamboo skewers, soaked
  in water for 30 minutes

Meat

Lamb biryani

Cook the rice following the packet instructions, adding the peas for the last 5 minutes of the cooking time. Then drain.

Meanwhile, heat the oil in a saucepan, and sauté the onion and ginger until softened. Add the spices, raisins, butter, mango chutney and lamb, and cook for 4–5 minutes.

Stir in the rice and peas, and sprinkle with flaked almonds, if using.

✎ 5 MINUTES

▦ 10 MINUTES

☺ 4–6 PORTIONS

✻ NOT SUITABLE FOR FREEZING

225 g (8 oz) basmati rice
150 g (5 oz) frozen peas
2 tablespoons sunflower oil
1 large onion, peeled and
    chopped
1 teaspoon grated fresh root
    ginger
½ teaspoon garam masala
¼ teaspoon turmeric
25 g (1 oz) raisins
25 g (1 oz) butter
1 tablespoon mango
    chutney
350 g (12 oz) cooked lamb,
    chopped
flaked almonds, to garnish
    (optional)

This is the perfect way to use up any lamb left over from the Sunday roast. It makes a wonderfully aromatic meal for a Monday evening.

Roast leg of lamb with roast potatoes

🔪 15 MINUTES, PLUS 1 HOUR FOR MARINATING

⏲ 2 HOURS 20 MINUTES

🍽 6 PORTIONS

❄ NOT SUITABLE FOR FREEZING

1.7 kg (3¾ lb) leg of lamb
2 garlic cloves, sliced
150 ml (¼ pint) red wine
1 tablespoon chopped thyme
2 tablespoons olive oil
salt and pepper
1 kg (2 lb 3 oz) King Edward
    potatoes, peeled and cut
    into medium-size chunks
3 tablespoons sunflower oil
1 tablespoon thyme leaves

Gravy
15 g (½ oz) butter
2 tablespoons plain flour
300 ml (½ pint) chicken stock
1 teaspoon Worcestershire
    sauce
2 teaspoons redcurrant jelly
½ teaspoon gravy browning

Make a few holes in the lamb with a knife, and push a slice of garlic into each one. Place the lamb in a bowl, then pour over the wine and chopped thyme. Leave to marinate for at least 1 hour.

Preheat the oven to 220°C/430°F/Gas 7. Transfer the lamb to a roasting tin, reserving the marinade. Drizzle over the olive oil and season well. Roast for 20 minutes, then reduce the temperature to 180°C/350°F/Gas 4. Cook the lamb for 25 minutes per 500 g (1 lb 2 oz).

Put the potatoes into cold water, then bring to the boil and cook for 5 minutes. Then drain.

Increase the oven temperature to 220°C/430°F/Gas 7. Heat a baking tray until hot. Add the sunflower oil, then the potatoes and thyme leaves. Roast for 25–35 minutes until golden and crisp, turning halfway through.

To make the gravy, melt the butter in a saucepan. Add the flour, then blend in the stock, Worcestershire sauce, redcurrant jelly and gravy browning. Stir until smooth and thickened. Mix in the lamb juices and sieve into a jug.

Spaghetti Bolognese

5 MINUTES

1 HOUR

4–6 PORTIONS

SUITABLE FOR FREEZING

1 tablespoon olive oil
1 large red onion, peeled
   and chopped
2 garlic cloves, crushed
500 g (1 lb 2 oz) lean minced
   beef
150 ml (¼ pint) red wine
800 g (28 oz) tinned
   chopped tomatoes
2 tablespoons tomato purée
1 teaspoon brown sugar
1 tablespoon Worcestershire
   sauce
1 tablespoon chopped
   thyme
salt and pepper
350 g (12 oz) spaghetti
Parmesan cheese, grated,
   to serve (optional)

Heat the oil in a large saucepan, add the onion and fry for 3 minutes, then add the garlic, followed by the minced beef. Fry until the mince has browned. Add the remaining ingredients (except the spaghetti and Parmesan, if using) and bring to the boil, then cover and simmer for 45 minutes, until the beef is tender.

Cook the spaghetti according to the packet instructions, then drain and mix with the sauce.

Serve with Parmesan cheese, if using.

Red onions contain higher levels of a photochemical called quercetin than regular brown onions. Studies suggest that quercetin helps to keep the heart healthy by preventing 'bad' cholesterol from being deposited in the arteries.

Tasty beefburgers

Heat the oil and sauté the onion for about 5 minutes, or until softened. In a mixing bowl, combine the onion with all the remaining ingredients, except for the flour, margarine and Marmite.

With floured hands, form the mixture into 8 burgers. Preheat the grill to High. Place the burgers on the grill pan or a foil-lined baking sheet. Dot with the margarine and Marmite, and grill for about 4 minutes on each side, or until cooked through.

Alternatively, heat a little oil in a shallow frying pan and fry the burgers for about 3 minutes on each side, until cooked through.

To freeze, put the uncooked burgers on a baking sheet lined with clingfilm. When frozen, individually wrap each one in clingfilm so that they can be defrosted as and when you need them.

15 MINUTES

15 MINUTES

8 BURGERS

SUITABLE FOR FREEZING

1 tablespoon vegetable oil
1 onion, peeled and finely chopped
400 g (14 oz) lean minced beef
1 tablespoon chopped parsley
1 chicken stock cube, finely crumbled
1 apple, peeled, cored and grated
1 egg, lightly beaten
50 g (2 oz) fresh breadcrumbs
1 teaspoon Worcestershire sauce
salt and pepper
a little plain flour, for shaping
a little margarine and Marmite, for grilling

Hungarian goulash

Preheat the oven to 180°C/350°F/Gas 4. Heat the oil in a frying pan and brown the beef on all sides, then transfer to a plate.

Put the onion and red pepper in the frying pan and fry for 3–4 minutes. Add the garlic, paprika and tomato purée and fry for another 2 minutes. Return the beef to the pan and coat in the onion mixture. Add the stock and bring to the boil. Cover with the lid and place in the oven for 1 hour. (If you don't have an ovenproof frying pan, you could use a casserole dish.)

Remove the pan from the oven and add the remaining ingredients. Put the pan on the hob and bring the goulash back to the boil, then cover and return to the oven for 30–40 minutes, or until the beef is tender. Serve with rice or mashed potato.

✏️ 5 MINUTES
🖵 1 HOUR 50 MINUTES
🕰 4 PORTIONS
❄️ SUITABLE FOR FREEZING

1 tablespoon sunflower oil
500 g (1 lb 2 oz) braising or stewing beef, cut into pieces
1 large onion, peeled and sliced
1 red pepper, deseeded and diced
2 garlic cloves, crushed
1 tablespoon paprika
1½ tablespoons tomato purée
400 ml (14 fl oz) beef stock
1½ teaspoons balsamic vinegar
½ teaspoon brown sugar
½ teaspoon mushroom ketchup
6 tablespoons full-fat crème fraîche

Sesame beef stir-fry

🔪 10 MINUTES

🍳 15–20 MINUTES

🍽 4 PORTIONS

❄ SUITABLE FOR FREEZING

1 tablespoon sesame oil
1 garlic clove, crushed
1 medium carrot, peeled and
   cut into matchsticks
100 g (3½ oz) baby corn,
   quartered
1 medium courgette, cut
   into matchsticks
300 g (11 oz) beef fillet, or
   rump steak, cut into very
   fine strips
1 tablespoon cornflour
1 tablespoon water
150 ml (¼ pint) beef stock
2 tablespoons dark brown
   sugar
2 tablespoons soy sauce
a few drops of Tabasco
   sauce
1 tablespoon sesame seeds

Heat the sesame oil in a wok and stir-fry the garlic,
carrot, baby corn and courgette for 3–4 minutes.
Add the beef and continue to stir-fry for another
4–5 minutes.

Mix the cornflour with the water and stir into
the beef stock. Stir this into the pan together
with the sugar, soy sauce, Tabasco and sesame
seeds. Bring to a simmer and cook until slightly
thickened. Serve with rice.

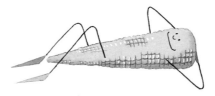

*I usually make this recipe using tail fillet. This is
slightly cheaper than a regular fillet steak, but has
exactly the same flavour and soft texture.*

Winter beef casserole

🖊 10 MINUTES

🕒 2 HOURS

🍴 4–6 PORTIONS

❄ SUITABLE FOR FREEZING

3 tablespoons sunflower oil
750 g (1 lb 10 oz) braising
 beef, cut into pieces
2 onions, peeled and
 chopped
2 medium carrots, peeled
 and chopped
2 garlic cloves, crushed
30 g (1 oz) plain flour
200 ml (7 fl oz) red wine
300 ml (½ pint) beef stock
1 tablespoon chopped
 thyme
1 tablespoon redcurrant jelly
1 tablespoon Worcestershire
 sauce
1 tablespoon sun-dried
 tomato paste
2 bay leaves
150 g (5 oz) button
 mushrooms, halved

Preheat the oven to 160°C/320°F/Gas 3. Heat
2 tablespoons of the oil in a hob-safe casserole
dish, and fry the beef in two batches, until
browned. Remove and set aside.

Heat the remaining oil, add the onion and
carrot and fry for 2 minutes. Add the garlic and
fry for another 30 seconds. Sprinkle over the flour,
then blend in the wine, stock, thyme, redcurrant
jelly, Worcestershire sauce, tomato paste and bay
leaves. Return the beef to the dish and bring to the
boil. Cover and transfer to the oven for 1½–2 hours,
until tender. Add the mushrooms for the last
20 minutes of the cooking time.

*Iron deficiency is the most common nutritional
deficiency in children in the UK. Red meat provides
the richest source of iron so, provided you're not
raising your child as a vegetarian, it's important
to include red meat in your child's diet.*

Cheesy cottage pie

Heat the oil in a large frying pan and fry the onion and carrot for 2 minutes. Add the mince and cook for a few minutes, until browned. Add the flour, then blend in the wine, stock, thyme, bay leaves, Worcestershire sauce, tomato purée, sugar and soy sauce. Bring to the boil, then cover and simmer for 45 minutes to 1 hour, until the meat and vegetables are tender. Preheat the oven to 200°C/400°F/Gas 6.

While the meat and vegetables are cooking, prepare the mashed potato. Cook the potatoes in boiling salted water for 10–15 minutes, until tender. Drain, then mash and stir in the milk, butter and half of the cheese. Season to taste.

Add seasoning to the meat and vegetables, then spoon into a shallow ovenproof dish. Spoon the mashed potato on top, and fluff up with a fork. Sprinkle with the remaining cheese. Put the cottage pie in the oven for 20 minutes, until bubbling and golden brown.

✑ 20 MINUTES

▦ 75–90 MINUTES

◷ 4–6 PORTIONS

❋ SUITABLE FOR FREEZING

1 tablespoon olive oil
2 onions, peeled and chopped
1 carrot, peeled and chopped
500 g (1 lb 2 oz) minced beef
30 g (1 oz) plain flour
150 ml (¼ pint) red wine
350 ml (12 fl oz) beef stock
1 tablespoon chopped thyme
2 bay leaves
1 tablespoon Worcestershire sauce
1 tablespoon tomato purée
a pinch of sugar
2 teaspoons soy sauce
1 kg (2 lb 3 oz) potatoes, peeled and cut into chunks
a little milk, for mashing
a knob of butter
125 g (4½ oz) Gruyère cheese, grated
salt and pepper

Cornish pasties

Heat the oil in a large saucepan and add the mince. Cook for a few minutes, until browned. Add the onion and carrot, and fry for another 5 minutes. Add the stock, Worcestershire sauce, tomato purée and thyme. Bring to the boil, then cover and simmer gently for 20 minutes, until the beef and vegetables are tender and the liquid has been absorbed. Add the potato, tomato ketchup and water, then season and leave to cool.

Meanwhile, roll out the pastry until thin. Cut out 4 circles, 15 cm (6 in) in diameter. You could use an upturned bowl or plate as a guide.

Preheat the oven to 220°C/430°F/Gas 7. Mix the Cheddar into the filling, then spoon a good quantity of the mixture into the middle of each pastry circle. Brush the edges with the egg. Bring the sides together and crimp the edges along the top, to seal. Brush with more egg, and make a hole in the top of each pasty to allow the steam to escape during cooking. If you have time, chill the pasties before cooking.

Place the pasties on a baking sheet and put in the oven for 15–20 minutes, until golden brown and puffy. Serve warm.

🔪 15 MINUTES, PLUS CHILLING
🗔 20 MINUTES
🍽 4 PORTIONS
❄ SUITABLE FOR FREEZING

1 tablespoon sunflower oil
250 g (9 oz) lean minced beef
1 large onion, peeled and chopped
1 medium carrot, peeled and finely diced
150 ml (¼ pint) beef stock
1 teaspoon Worcestershire sauce
½ teaspoon tomato purée
½ teaspoon chopped thyme
75 g (3 oz) cooked potato, diced
2 teaspoons tomato ketchup
4 tablespoons cold water
salt and pepper
250 g (9 oz) puff pastry
40 g (1½ oz) mature Cheddar cheese, grated
1 egg, beaten, to glaze

Sticky barbecue ribs

10 MINUTES

1 HOUR 10 MINUTES

4–6 PORTIONS

NOT SUITABLE FOR FREEZING

1.25 kg (2 lb 12 oz) spare ribs
salt and pepper, to season

Barbecue sauce
1 tablespoon olive oil
1 small red onion, peeled
   and chopped
1 garlic clove, crushed
150 ml (¼ pint) tomato
   ketchup
100 ml (3½ fl oz) freshly
   squeezed orange juice
4 tablespoons clear honey
1 tablespoon dark soy sauce
2 teaspoons Worcestershire
   sauce

Preheat the oven to 170°C/325°F/Gas 3. Heat the oil in a frying pan, and sauté the onion for 5 minutes, until softened. Add the garlic and cook for 1 minute, then add the remaining ingredients for the sauce. Bring to the boil, then simmer for 1 minute. Allow to cool slightly, then transfer to a blender and whiz until smooth.

Line a large roasting tin with aluminium foil (for easier clean-up), and put in the spare ribs. Season with salt and pepper, then pour over the barbecue sauce and toss to coat the ribs. Cover with more foil and put in the oven for 30 minutes.

Turn the oven up to 200°C/400°F/Gas 6, uncover the ribs and cook for another 30 minutes, turning over halfway through. Transfer to a plate and allow to cool slightly before serving.

Alternatively, you can grill or barbecue the ribs. Cook, uncoated, under a medium-hot grill, or over medium-hot coals, for 10 minutes on each side. Then turn and brush the ribs with some of the sauce. Grill or barbecue for 5 minutes, then turn and brush with more sauce. Repeat 3–4 times until the ribs are cooked through, with a sticky coating. These are great served with jacket potatoes.

Sausage and prawn paella

Put the rice into a saucepan of boiling water and add the stock cube. Cook according to the packet instructions, then drain well.

While the rice is cooking, heat the oil in a saucepan and sauté the onion for 5 minutes. Add the garlic and fry for another 30 seconds. Add the vinegar and stir until reduced. Then add the peas and cook for a couple of minutes, stirring constantly, then add the prawns and rice. Toss together, then add the sausage, tomato, lemon juice, thyme and seasoning. Stir over the heat for a few minutes, to heat through, then serve.

🔪 7 MINUTES
📅 20 MINUTES
🍽 4 PORTIONS
❄ SUITABLE FOR FREEZING

225 g (8 oz) basmati rice
1 chicken stock cube
2 tablespoons sunflower oil
2 onions, peeled and finely chopped
2 garlic cloves, crushed
2 tablespoons white wine vinegar
50 g (2 oz) frozen peas
100 g (3½ oz) small cooked prawns
75 g (3 oz) cooked sausage, sliced
3 tomatoes, deseeded and chopped
2 teaspoons lemon juice
1 teaspoon thyme leaves
salt and pepper

Prawns are an excellent source of vitamin B12, which is necessary for the formation of blood cells and nerves.

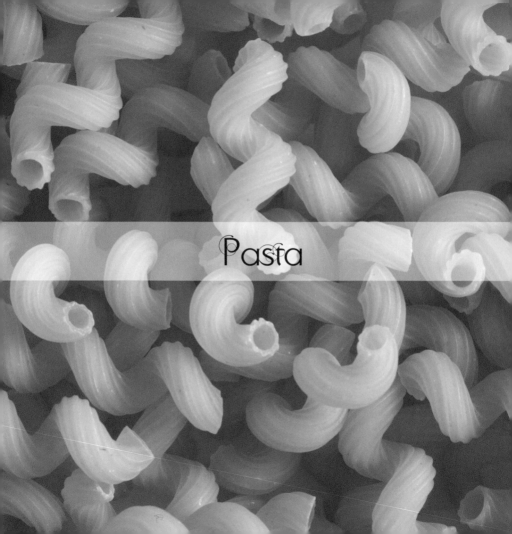

Pasta

Sausage, sage and red onion fusilli

Cook the fusilli following the packet instructions.

Heat the oil in a saucepan and sauté the onion until softened. Add the honey and brown sugar and cook for 10 minutes, until caramelized.

Heat a little oil in a frying pan and add the sausages. Turn regularly until cooked through, then slice.

Mix together the pasta, caramelized onion, sausages and sage. Season to taste, then serve.

5 MINUTES

25 MINUTES

4 PORTIONS

SUITABLE FOR FREEZING

160 g (5½ oz) fusilli pasta
2 tablespoons sunflower oil
300 g (11 oz) red onion,
    peeled and sliced
1 tablespoon honey
20 g (¾ oz) brown sugar
8 Cumberland or
    Lincolnshire sausages
10 sage leaves, chopped
salt and pepper

Pasta is a good source of complex carbohydrate, which provides us with sustained energy. Try mixing some wholemeal pasta with regular pasta to increase the fibre content of the meal.

Stir-fried beef with noodles

⟋ 20 MINUTES

☐ 15–20 MINUTES

🍳 4 PORTIONS

❄ NOT SUITABLE FOR FREEZING

300 g (11 oz) sirloin, rump or
  fillet steak
2 eggs
4 tablespoons cornflour
a pinch of salt
100 g (3½ oz) medium egg
  noodles
1 medium carrot, peeled and
  cut into matchsticks
2 medium courgettes,
  peeled and cut into
  matchsticks
sunflower oil, for frying
4 spring onions, sliced
1 red chilli, deseeded and
  chopped
1 garlic clove, crushed

Sauce

3 tablespoons rice vinegar
2 tablespoons soy sauce
1 teaspoon cornflour
3 tablespoons chicken stock
  or water
2½ tablespoons caster sugar

Cut the beef into thin slices, across the grain, then stack a few slices on top of each other and cut into slivers the size of long matchsticks. Whisk the eggs with the cornflour and salt, to make a batter. Add the meat and stir well to coat. Cook the noodles following the packet instructions.

Quarter-fill a large wok with oil. Heat, and when just beginning to smoke, add the carrot and courgette and stir-fry for 1 minute. Remove and transfer to a dish lined with kitchen paper. Reheat the oil and, when starting to smoke, add half of the beef, using tongs to ensure the strips remain separate. Fry until crispy (3–5 minutes), then drain, and add to the carrot and courgettes. Repeat with the remaining beef.

Clean out the wok, heat 1 tablespoon of oil, then add the spring onions, chilli and garlic. Stir-fry for a few seconds, then add the noodles.

To make the sauce, mix together the vinegar and soy sauce in a small bowl. In another, blend the cornflour and stock or water. Combine the two mixtures and add the caster sugar. Add to the noodles, then toss with the beef and vegetables. Stir-fry briefly until heated through.

Beef stroganoff with tagliatelle

✎ 15 MINUTES

▭ 25 MINUTES

◔ 4 PORTIONS

❄ SUITABLE FOR FREEZING
(STROGANOFF ONLY)

Heat 2 teaspoons of oil in a wok or large frying pan and sauté the mushrooms for 5–6 minutes, until golden brown. Transfer to a bowl. Heat 1 teaspoon of oil in the wok or pan and fry the steak quickly (1–2 minutes), until browned. Don't overcrowd the pan – it's best to cook the meat in 2 or 3 batches; otherwise the beef will stew in its own juices. Transfer the beef to the bowl with the mushrooms.

Reduce the heat to low. Melt the butter and gently cook the shallots for 8–10 minutes, until softened. Add the garlic and thyme, and cook for 1 minute. Turn up the heat, add the stock and boil for 2–3 minutes, until reduced by half. Whisk in the cream, mustard, soy sauce and sugar and boil for another 2–3 minutes, until thick enough to coat the back of a spoon. Reduce the heat again, and add the mushrooms and beef. Add black pepper and lemon juice to taste.

Cook the tagliatelle according to the packet instructions. Drain and transfer to plates. Spoon over the sauce. Garnish with thyme, and serve.

olive oil, for frying
150 g (5 oz) mushrooms
  (button, chestnut or
  shiitake), thinly sliced
225 g (8 oz) fillet or sirloin
  steak, thinly sliced
a large knob of butter
3 small shallots, peeled and
  thinly sliced
1 garlic clove, crushed
½ teaspoon thyme leaves,
  plus extra to garnish
250 ml (8 fl oz) beef stock
200 ml (7 fl oz) double cream
½ teaspoon Dijon mustard
2 teaspoons soy sauce
1 teaspoon sugar
freshly ground black
  pepper, to taste
small squeeze of lemon
  juice, to taste
200 g (7 oz) tagliatelle

Pesto spaghetti with roasted peppers

⏱ 5 MINUTES

🍳 15 MINUTES

👥 3–4 PORTIONS

❄ NOT SUITABLE FOR FREEZING

50 g (2 oz) pine nuts
1 garlic clove, peeled and chopped or sliced
25 g (1 oz) basil
50 g (2 oz) Parmesan cheese, grated, plus extra to serve
100 ml (3½ fl oz) olive oil
a pinch of sugar
salt and pepper
250 g (9 oz) spaghetti
100 g (3½ oz) roasted peppers (from a jar), chopped
2 tablespoons double cream

First, make the pesto. Put the pine nuts in a small, dry frying pan and toast until golden. Allow to cool, then transfer to a jug with the garlic, basil, Parmesan, olive oil and sugar. Blend until smooth, using an electric hand blender. Season to taste.

Cook the spaghetti according to the packet instructions, then drain, reserving 50 ml (2 fl oz) of the cooking water.

Put the pesto, roasted peppers, cream and reserved water into a saucepan and heat through. Add the spaghetti and toss until well coated. Add more seasoning if needed, and serve with extra Parmesan.

Basil can aid digestion, easing the symptoms of wind, stomach cramps and indigestion.

Vegetable lasagne

Preheat the oven to 220°C/430°F/Gas 7. Heat the oil in a saucepan, add the onions and fry for 5 minutes, until softened. Add the pepper, courgette and aubergine, fry for 5 minutes, then stir in the garlic. Add the tinned tomatoes, tomato purée and oregano, then bring to the boil and simmer for 20 minutes. Season to taste.

While the vegetables are cooking, make the sauce. Melt the butter in a saucepan, stir in the flour, then blend in the milk and stir until thickened and smooth. Mix in the mustard and half of the cheese, until the cheese has melted.

Put one third of the vegetable sauce into an ovenproof dish. Top with 2 sheets of lasagne and a third of the cheese sauce. Repeat until you have three layers. Sprinkle the remaining cheese on top.

Bake for 30 minutes, until the top is bubbling and golden .

🖊 15 MINUTES

🗔 1 HOUR

⏲ 4–6 PORTIONS

❄ SUITABLE FOR FREEZING

1 tablespoon olive oil
2 small onions, peeled and sliced
1 yellow pepper, deseeded and chopped
1 courgette, chopped
½ aubergine, topped and tailed, and chopped
2 garlic cloves, crushed
800 g (28 oz) tinned chopped tomatoes
2 tablespoons tomato purée
½ teaspoon chopped oregano
salt and pepper
6 sheets fresh lasagne

Cheese sauce
40 g (1½ oz) butter
40 g (1½ oz) plain flour
600 ml (1 pint) milk
1 teaspoon Dijon mustard
100 g (3½ oz) Cheddar cheese, grated

Salmon, prawn and dill lasagne

/ 30 MINUTES

📺 50 MINUTES

🍽 4 PORTIONS

❄ SUITABLE FOR FREEZING

50 g (2 oz) butter
1 leek, finely chopped
1½ teaspoons white wine
 vinegar
50 g (2 oz) plain flour
600 ml (1 pint) milk
2 tablespoons lemon juice
100 g (3½ oz) baby spinach
2 tablespoons chopped dill
80 g (3 oz) Parmesan cheese,
 grated
salt and pepper
300 g (11 oz) salmon fillet,
 skinned and cut into
 2 cm (¾ in) cubes
225 g (8 oz) cooked king
 prawns
150 g (5 oz) broccoli, cut into
 small florets and blanched
4 sheets lasagne

Preheat the oven to 200°C/400°F/Gas 6. Melt
the butter in a deep saucepan, add the leek and
sauté over a low heat for 5–6 minutes, until
softened. Add the vinegar, then stir in the flour
until blended. Add the milk, bring to the boil, then
stir until thickened. Add the lemon juice, spinach,
dill and 50 g (2 oz) of the Parmesan. Stir over the
heat until the spinach has wilted. Season to taste.

Put a third of the salmon, prawns and broccoli
into the base of a small ovenproof dish (about
21 x 16 x 7 cm/8¼ x 6¼ x 2¾ in). Pour over a third
of the sauce. Place 2 sheets of lasagne on top.
Repeat, then finish with a layer of the fish
mixture and sauce. Sprinkle with the remaining
Parmesan, then put the lasagne in the oven for
30 minutes. Leave to stand for 5 minutes before
serving.

Marina's spaghetti with seafood

🔪 18 MINUTES

🍳 25 MINUTES

🍽 4 PORTIONS

❄ NOT SUITABLE FOR FREEZING

Discard any mussels or clams that open when gently pressed. Place the remainder in a bowl of salt water for 10 minutes, to extract any sand caught in the shells. If the shells still feel gritty, scrub them under cold running water, using a stiff brush. Wipe the shells clean using damp kitchen paper. Cut any beards (little fibrous tufts) from the mussels using a knife or scissors. Place the mussels and clams in a colander and give them a final rinse before using. If you're not using them straight away, store in the fridge.

Heat the oil in a large saucepan and fry the onion and garlic for 7–8 minutes, until soft. Add the Noilly Prat or wine, if using, bring to the boil and reduce by half. Add the tomatoes, stock, Tabasco, sugar and seasoning, and cook for 10 minutes.

Meanwhile, cook the spaghetti according to the packet instructions, then drain.

Add all the seafood and basil to the tomato sauce, stir well, cover and cook for 3–4 minutes. Then stir in the spaghetti and lemon juice just before serving.

500 g (1 lb 2 oz) mussels
250 g (9 oz) clams
2 tablespoons olive oil
1 red onion, peeled and
   sliced
1 garlic clove, crushed
50 ml (2 fl oz) Noilly Prat
   or white wine (optional)
400 g (14 oz) tinned
   chopped tomatoes
100 ml (3½ fl oz) fish stock
a few drops of Tabasco
   sauce
1 teaspoon sugar
salt and pepper
200 g (7 oz) spaghetti
250 g (9 oz) large fresh
   prawns, peeled, and heads
   and veins removed
1 tablespoon chopped basil
1 tablespoon lemon juice

Dessert

Mini bread and butter puddings

Spread one side of each slice of bread with butter and jam. Remove the crusts, then cut each slice into 4 triangles. Arrange the triangles in 4 ramekins (about 10 cm/4 in in diameter) and scatter over the sultanas.

In a jug, combine the egg, vanilla extract, double cream, milk and caster sugar, then pour into the ramekins. Sprinkle over the demerara sugar and leave the puddings to stand for 20 minutes. Preheat the oven to 200°C/400°F/Gas 6.

Bake the puddings for 20 minutes, until puffy and lightly golden brown. Serve straight away.

15 MINUTES, PLUS 20 MINUTES FOR STANDING

20 MINUTES

4 PORTIONS

SUITABLE FOR FREEZING

4 small slices of white bread
25 g (1 oz) butter, softened
1 heaped tablespoon apricot jam
50 g (2 oz) sultanas
1 egg
1 teaspoon vanilla extract
150 ml (¼ pint) double cream
100 ml (3½ fl oz) milk
50 g (2 oz) caster sugar
2 tablespoons demerara sugar

Lemon soufflé pudding

/ 20 MINUTES

🖵 30 MINUTES

🍪 6 PORTIONS

❄️ NOT SUITABLE FOR FREEZING

100 g (3½ oz) butter,
    softened
100 g (3½ oz) caster sugar
4 eggs, separated
50 g (2 oz) plain flour
finely grated zest and juice
    of 2 large lemons
300 ml (½ pint) milk

Preheat the oven to 180°C/350°F/Gas 4. Grease
a 1.5 litre (2½ pint) ovenproof dish.

In a large bowl, whisk together the butter and
sugar until light and fluffy. Add the egg yolks,
flour, lemon zest and juice and whisk again.
Slowly add the milk to make a thick batter. It will
look curdled at this stage.

Whisk the egg whites until stiff, then fold into
the lemon batter. Pour into the prepared dish.
Bake for 30 minutes, until well risen and lightly
golden on top.

You could also make individual portions using
ramekins.

Apple tarte tatin

Preheat the oven to 220°C/430°F/Gas 7. Melt the butter in a saucepan. Add the sugar and stir until it turns to a dark golden brown. Pour the caramel into a deep sandwich tin or tarte tatin tin, 20 cm (8 in) in diameter.

Toss the apples in the lemon juice, then arrange on top of the caramel.

Roll out the pastry to make a circle slightly larger than the base of the tin. Place it on top of the apples, then trim off the excess pastry. Press down the sides.

Bake the tarte tatin for 30–35 minutes, until the pastry is golden and crisp. Turn upside down onto a plate, and serve with ice cream.

/ 15 MINUTES

☐ 35–40 MINUTES

🍪 6 PORTIONS

❄ NOT SUITABLE FOR FREEZING

100 g (3½ oz) butter
100 g (3½ oz) light brown
   sugar
5 Pink Lady apples, peeled,
   cored and thinly sliced
juice of ½ a lemon
300 g (11 oz) puff pastry
vanilla ice cream, to serve
   (optional)

Pancakes with strawberries and toffee

⟋ 20 MINUTES

▦ 45 MINUTES

◉ 8 PANCAKES

❄ SUITABLE FOR FREEZING

15 g (½ oz) caster sugar
150 g (5 oz) plain flour
2 eggs
250 ml (8 fl oz) milk
2 tablespoons sunflower oil
125 g (4½ oz) light cream
  cheese
200 g (7 oz) strawberries,
  hulled and sliced

Toffee sauce
50 g (2 oz) butter
50 g (2 oz) light brown sugar
150 ml (¼ pint) double
  cream
½ teaspoon vanilla essence

You can make the pancakes in advance and freeze, or keep them in the fridge for a couple of days. To store, separate them with greaseproof paper and cover with clingfilm..

Put the sugar and flour into a large bowl, make a well in the centre, then add the eggs. Gradually add the milk, and whisk until smooth.

Heat a little oil in a small omelette pan. Pour in a little batter, tilt to coat the base of the pan and cook for 2–3 minutes. Carefully flip the pancake, then cook the other side. Slide it onto a plate. Repeat until you've used all the batter.

Place a pancake on a board, and spread a tablespoon of cream cheese around the centre. Arrange a few strawberry slices on top. Fold the sides into the middle, then fold in half lengthways, so you have a rough square shape. Repeat with the remaining pancakes.

To make the toffee sauce, melt the butter in a small saucepan, add the sugar and cream, and slowly bring to the boil. Remove from the heat and add the vanilla essence. Drizzle the sauce over the pancakes to serve.

Layered chocolate and raspberry mousse

Put the white chocolate into a small heatproof bowl and the milk chocolate in another. Heat over a pan of simmering water until melted, then set aside.

Whip the cream until just under soft-peak consistency, then divide into two bowls. Add the white chocolate to one bowl and the milk chocolate to the other. Gently fold in until well combined.

Put the raspberries and icing sugar into a jug and blend until smooth, using an electric hand blender. Sieve into a large bowl to remove the raspberry seeds.

In each glass or bowl, put a layer of milk chocolate mousse, followed by some raspberry coulis, then a layer of white chocolate mousse. Repeat the layers. Chill for at least 30 minutes before serving.

🔪 25 MINUTES, PLUS 30 MINUTES FOR CHILLING

🍳 10 MINUTES

🕐 6 PORTIONS

❄ SUITABLE FOR FREEZING

100 g (3½ oz) white chocolate
100 g (3½ oz) milk chocolate
300 ml (½ pint) whipping cream
150 g (5 oz) raspberries
2 tablespoons icing sugar
6 small glasses or glass bowls

Raspberry ripple cheesecake

✎ 45 MINUTES, PLUS CHILLING

▦ 12 MINUTES

☺ 8 PORTIONS

❄ NOT SUITABLE FOR FREEZING

7 gelatine leaves (about 12 g/
  ¼ oz) or 1 x 11 g (¼ oz) sachet
  powdered gelatine
200 g (7 oz) digestive
  biscuits, broken into pieces
100 g (3½ oz) butter
150 g (5 oz) fresh raspberries
2 tablespoons icing sugar
1 tablespoon cornflour
450 g (1 lb) cream cheese, at
  room temperature
225 g (8 oz) caster sugar
2 teaspoons vanilla extract
400 ml (14 fl oz) double
  cream, beaten until stiff
300 g (11 oz) fresh berries
  (such as raspberries,
  strawberries and
  blackberries) for topping
85 g (3 oz) white chocolate,
  melted
piping bag with small plain
  writing nozzle

Dissolve the gelatine according to the packet instructions. Set aside to cool. Put the biscuits in a plastic bag and crush with a rolling pin. Melt the butter in a large pan and stir in the crumbs. Spread over the base of a 20 cm (8 in) loose-bottomed cake tin, press down, then put in the fridge.

Blitz the raspberries and icing sugar. Sieve over a small pan. Mix 1 tablespoon of the coulis with the cornflour. Return to the pan and stir. Bring to the boil. Remove from the heat. Leave to cool and thicken up. Beat the cream cheese, caster sugar and vanilla, until smooth. Stir 6 tablespoonfuls into the gelatine. Fold into the cream cheese, together with the cream.

Spread half of the mixture over the biscuit base. Spoon half of the coulis on top, in blobs, using a skewer to make ripples. Spoon the remaining cheesecake mixture on top and spread carefully. Level the surface using a palette knife. Trail coulis across the top, then use a skewer to create a pattern. Refrigerate to set.

Place the berries on top. Spoon the chocolate into the piping bag and pipe zigzag lines over the fruit.

Chocolate fudge cake

Preheat the oven to 180°C/350°F/Gas 4. Line three 20 cm (8 in) sandwich tins with a disc of non-stick paper, and grease the sides.

Put all the cake ingredients (except for the plain chocolate, if using) into a large mixing bowl, then combine using an electric hand whisk. Spoon into the tins and level the surfaces. Bake for 25 minutes, until the sponges are well risen and the sides are coming away from the tins. Leave to cool.

Put all the ingredients for the chocolate buttercream icing into a bowl, then whisk until smooth. Cover the surface of two of the sponges with the icing, then sandwich all three sponges together.

Put the chocolate and cream into a heatproof bowl, set over a pan of simmering water. Stir until the chocolate has melted, then set aside to cool and thicken (don't put it in the fridge). When the ganache is thick enough, spread over the top of the cake. Decorate with chocolate curls, or any decoration of your choice.

🖊 40 MINUTES

⊞ 30 MINUTES

🍽 10 PORTIONS

❄ SUITABLE FOR FREEZING (SPONGES ONLY)

6 eggs
350 g (12 oz) butter, softened
350 g (12 oz) caster sugar
100 g (3½ oz) cocoa powder
250 g (9 oz) self-raising flour
3 teaspoons baking powder
plain chocolate, to decorate (optional)

Chocolate buttercream icing
70 g (2½ oz) butter, softened
30 g (1 oz) cocoa powder
4 tablespoons milk
250 g (9 oz) icing sugar

Chocolate ganache
100 g (3½ oz) plain chocolate, broken into pieces
100 ml ((3½ fl oz) double cream

Index

About Annabel Karmel

Mother of three, Annabel Karmel MBE is the UK's number one parenting author and expert on devising delicious, nutritious meals for babies, toddlers and children.

Since launching with *The Complete Baby and Toddler Meal Planner* more than two decades ago, Annabel has written 37 books, which have sold over 4 million copies worldwide, covering every stage of a child's development.

With the sole aim of helping parents give their children the very best start in life, Annabel's tried-and-tested recipes have also grown into a successful supermarket food range. From delicious Organic Baby Purées to her best-selling healthy chilled meals, these offer the goodness of a home-cooked meal for those busy days.

Annabel was awarded an MBE in 2006, in the Queen's Birthday Honours, for her outstanding work in child nutrition. She also has menus in some of the largest leisure resorts in Britain and a successful app, *Annabel's Essential Guide to Feeding Your Baby and Toddler*.

For more information and recipes, visit **www.annabelkarmel.com**.

Acknowledgements

Louise Ward and Phil Carroll (Sainsbury's Books), Fiona MacIntyre, Martin Higgins and Cat Dowlett (Ebury), Dave King (photography), Tamsin Weston (props), Kate Bliman and Maud Eden (food stylists), Lucinda McCord (recipe testing), Nick Eddison and Katie Golsby (Eddison Sadd), and Sarah Smith (PR).

annabel karmel

Other titles in the series are:

ANNABEL KARMEL'S FAVOURITES

First foods
Recipes and advice to help you wean your baby

Suitable from four months

ANNABEL KARMEL'S FAVOURITES

Exploring new tastes
Introduce your baby to new flavours and textures

Suitable from six to nine months

ANNABEL KARMEL'S FAVOURITES

Growing independence
Healthy home-made recipes to encourage self-feeding

Suitable from nine to twelve months

ANNABEL KARMEL'S FAVOURITES

Toddler meals
Nutritious recipes for your child to enjoy with the family

Suitable from one year

ANNABEL KARMEL'S FAVOURITES

Lunchboxes
Quick, easy and healthy ideas to make lunchtime fun

50 healthy recipes

ANNABEL KARMEL'S FAVOURITES

Tasty food for fussy kids
Great recipes to tempt your picky eater

50 healthy recipes

ANNABEL KARMEL'S FAVOURITES

Vegetarian meals
Delicious, nutritious recipes for veggie kids

50 healthy recipes

ANNABEL KARMEL'S FAVOURITES

Party food
Quick, quirky and fun ideas for your child's celebration

50 healthy recipes

ANNABEL KARMEL'S FAVOURITES

Kids in the Kitchen
Creative recipe ideas to make and bake together

50 healthy recipes